# Maple Tree

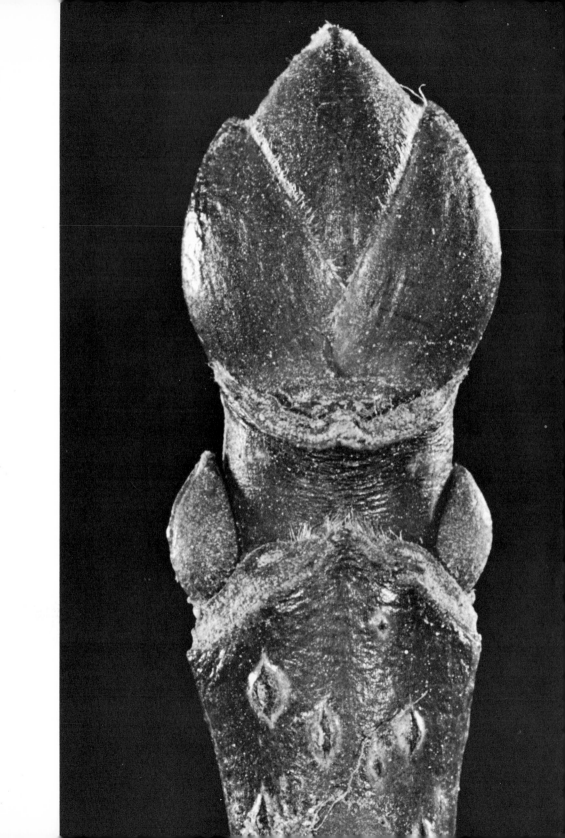

MILLICENT E. SELSAM

# Maple Tree

photographs by JEROME WEXLER

William Morrow and Company
New York

By the same author

DESIGN BY CYNTHIA BASIL

The author and photographer thank
Mr. Johnnie L. Gentry, Jr.
associated with the
New York Botanical Garden
for checking the text
and photographs of this book.

ACKNOWLEDGMENTS FOR PHOTOGRAPHS
Lynwood M. Chase of the National Audubon Society, 7, 10
United States Forest Service, 21, 22, 42
Field Museum of Natural History, 43
American Forest Products Industries, Inc., 44, 45

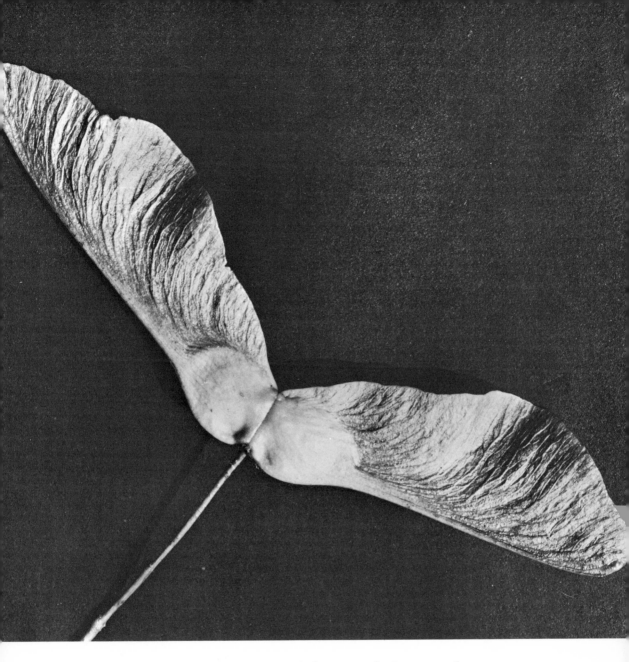

Do you know the winged fruits of the maple tree?

You can fly them through the air. You can put them on your nose.

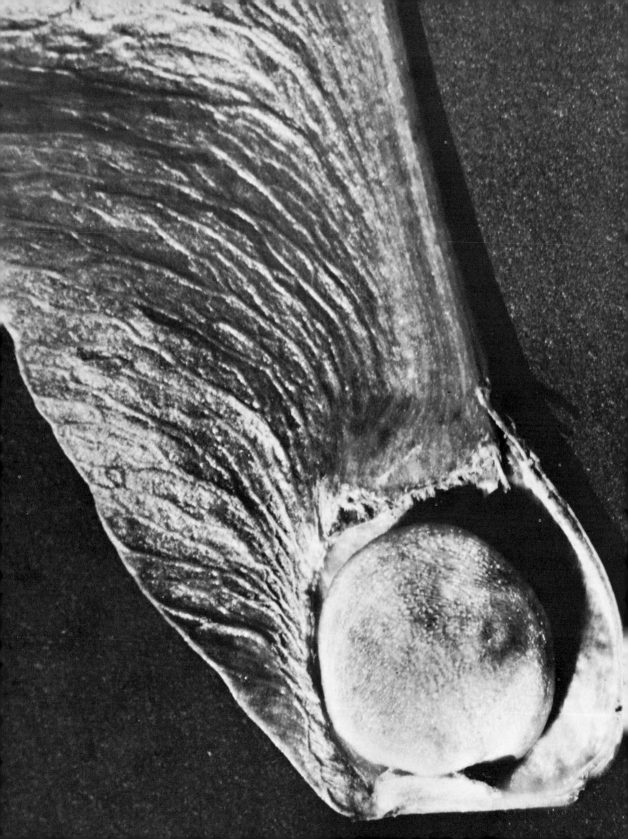

But maple fruits are not only toys. They are called fruits, because they contain seeds. Inside of them, at the bottom of each wing, is a seed that can grow into a new maple tree.

Here are maple fruits lying on the ground. The snow that covered them all winter is melting.

The ground is wet. The water enters the seed. It swells and cracks open. A root comes out of the seed. It goes into the ground.

Now the root is in the ground, and the wing is raised in the air. It is like a sign that reads, "Here a Maple Tree Is Growing."

The top part of the baby plant inside the seed is coming out.

This top part looks like crumpled leaves. They are called seed leaves, because they come from inside the seed. They provide food for the growing plant.

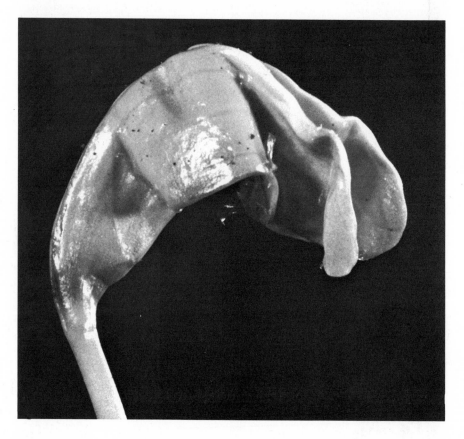

Now the seed leaves spread apart, and you can see a bud in the center. ▶

The bud opens into tiny little leaves.

The leaves unfold and grow bigger.

New buds keep opening into new leaves and stems. You can see that this young maple tree is growing in a flowerpot.

But other young maple trees are growing outside where the winged fruits fell.

As the tree grows, the trunk and branches become thicker. A growing layer, just inside the bark, adds new wood on the inside and new bark on the outside from year to year.

There is a separate ring of wood for each year. Count the rings on this pine tree to find how old it was when it was cut. As the tree trunk grows thicker, the bark splits on the outside.

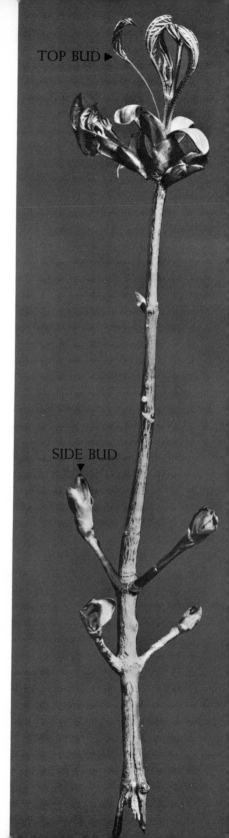

TOP BUD ▶

SIDE BUD
▼

A tree grows taller and taller, because every year new buds keep opening into new stems and leaves at the top of the tree. There are side buds too, and they grow out into the branches of the tree.

The young tree in front is about ten years old.
Notice the top growth and the branches.

Every summer new buds are formed. In the fall
the leaves turn yellow and fall off the trees, but
the buds remain on the tree all winter long.

Packed away inside the buds are tiny leaves and stems. When the tree is old enough, it produces flowers inside the buds too. The buds are protected all winter by thick, hard bud scales, which overlap each other like fish scales.

The ground warms up in the spring. Rains fall. Water enters the ground and goes into the roots of the trees. There it mixes with plant juices and becomes what is called sap. The sap rises to the tops of the trees and fills the buds.

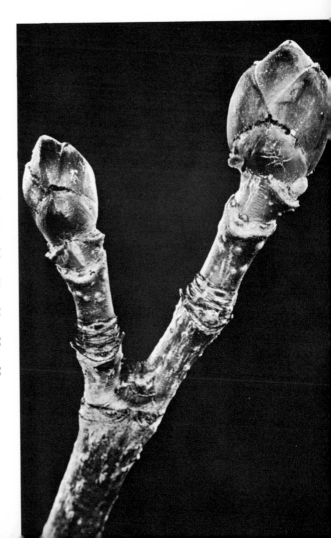

A bud is opening.
The inner hairy scales
are coming out.

Now the hairy scales
are opening.

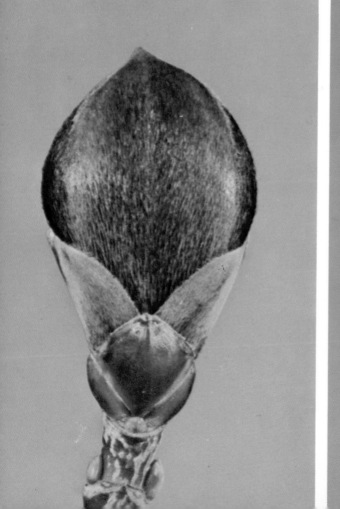
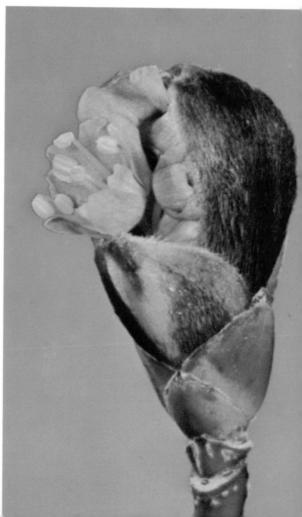

Flowers and leaves are coming out.

The stems and leaves and flowers that have come from the bud grow bigger.

The tree is in full flower.

There are two kinds of flowers on the maple tree. One kind has eight stamens that have pollen bags at the top. Can you count all eight stamens in the open flower?

Here are two stamens in a close-up view. You can see the dusty pollen in the pollen bags.

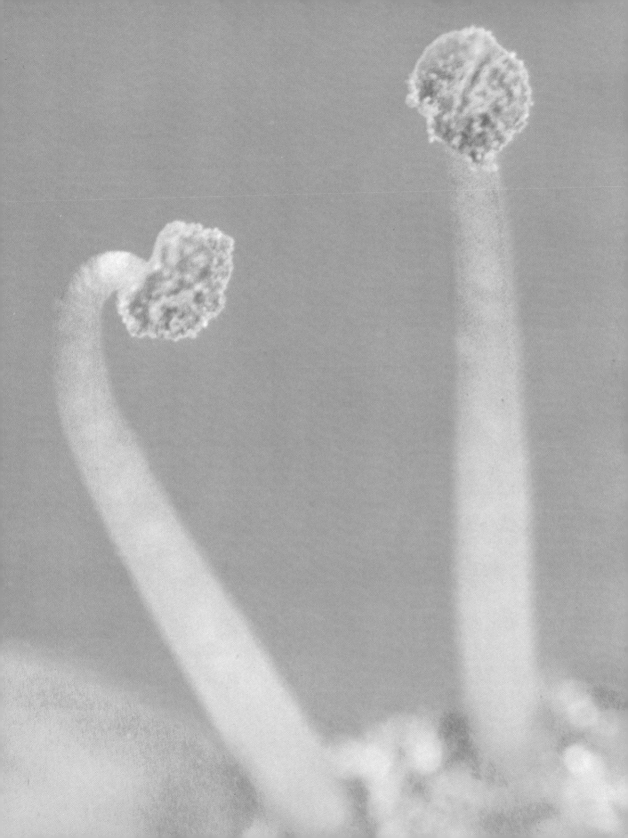

The other kind of flower has a center part, called the pistil, which can grow into a maple fruit. The pistil is divided in two at the top. The stamens around it are small. They never grow tall and produce pollen. Here the petals are pulled off so that you can see the inner parts of the flower.

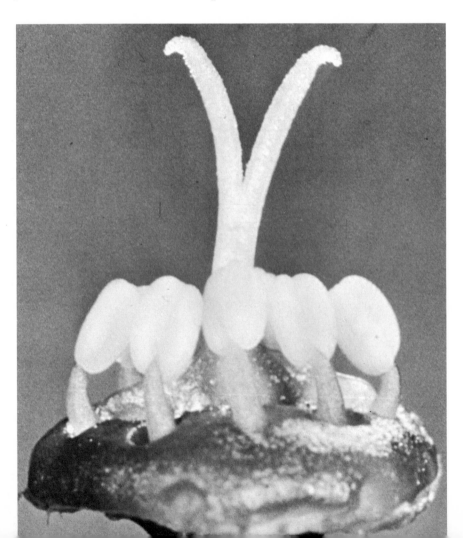

The front stamens have been clipped away here, so that you can see the bottom of the pistil, called the ovary. It already has two thin wings. Inside are ovules, or seeds-to-be. They become seeds only if they are fertilized, that is, if they are joined by the contents of a pollen grain.

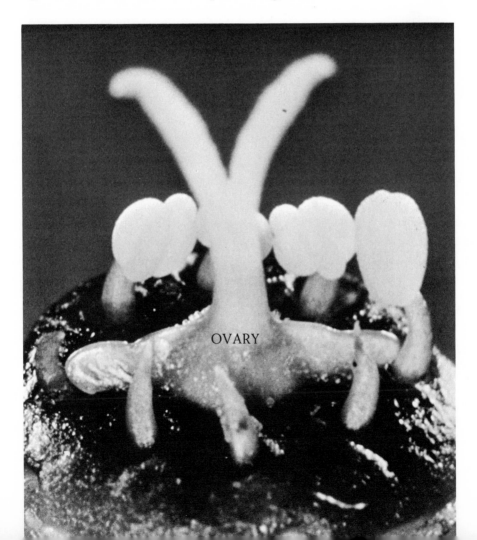

The flowers are sweet, and insects come to suck the flower juice, which is called nectar. When they land on the flowers with stamens, they get dusted with pollen. When they fly to the flowers with pistils they accidentally brush off the pollen grains onto the top part of the pistil.

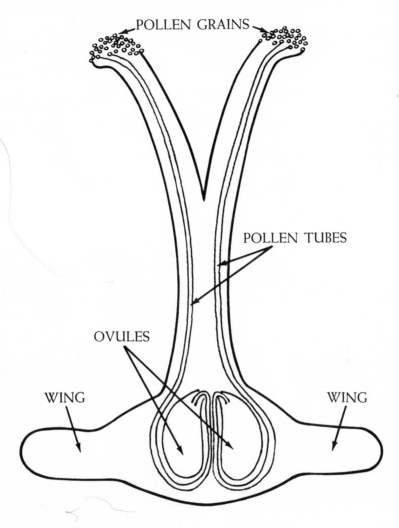

POLLEN GRAINS

POLLEN TUBES

OVULES

WING

WING

The pollen grains send out tubes that grow down to the ovary, where the ovules are. The contents of each pollen tube join with an ovule. The ovules are fertilized and now will change into seeds.

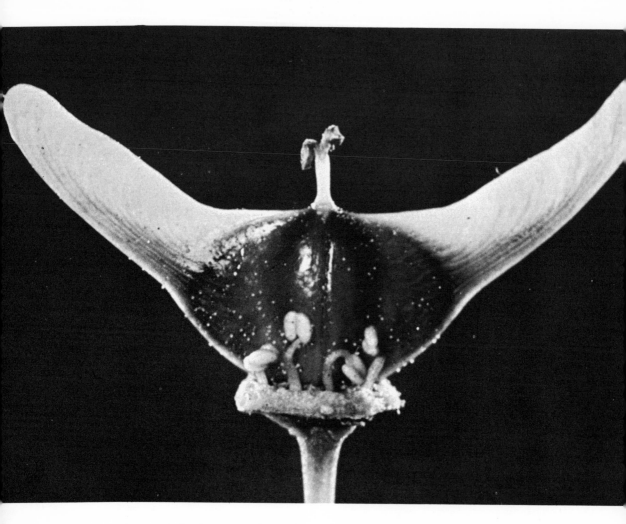

Around the ovules the ovary will enlarge into the winged fruit.

The fruits grow all summer and ripen in the fall.
They get heavier and turn down toward the
ground. Notice how big the wings are now. Some
people call them coat hangers. You can see why.

When fall comes, the wind shakes the fruits from the tree. The large wings help to keep these fruits in the air. They whirl around and around as the wind carries them. In this way, some are blown far from the tree. Other fruits hang on to the maple tree during the winter. By spring they, too, have fallen to the ground. The fruits split along the center line into two sections, each with one wing and one seed.

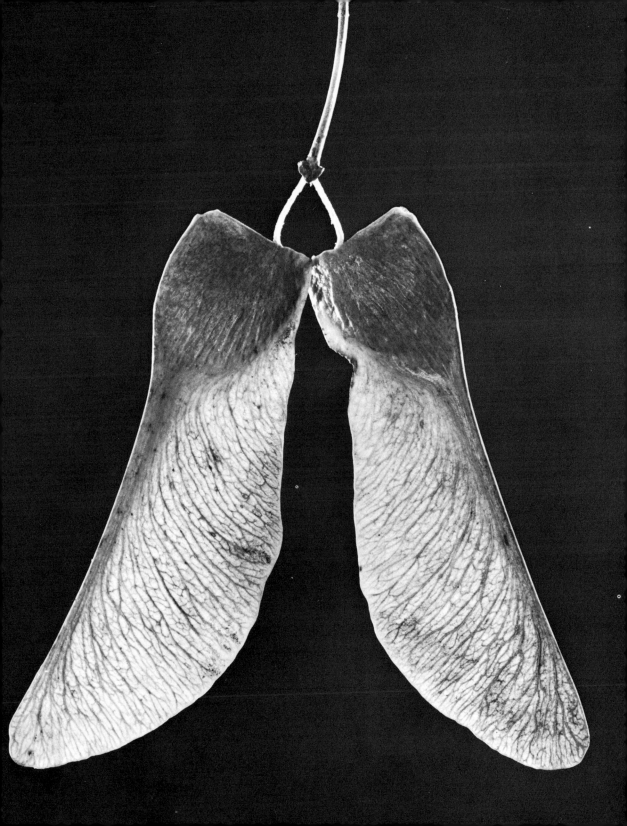

New maple seeds sprout wherever they lie.

Some will grow into big maple trees.

NORWAY MAPLE

This story tells about one kind of maple tree, the Norway maple. There are also other kinds of maples, and they grow in the same way.

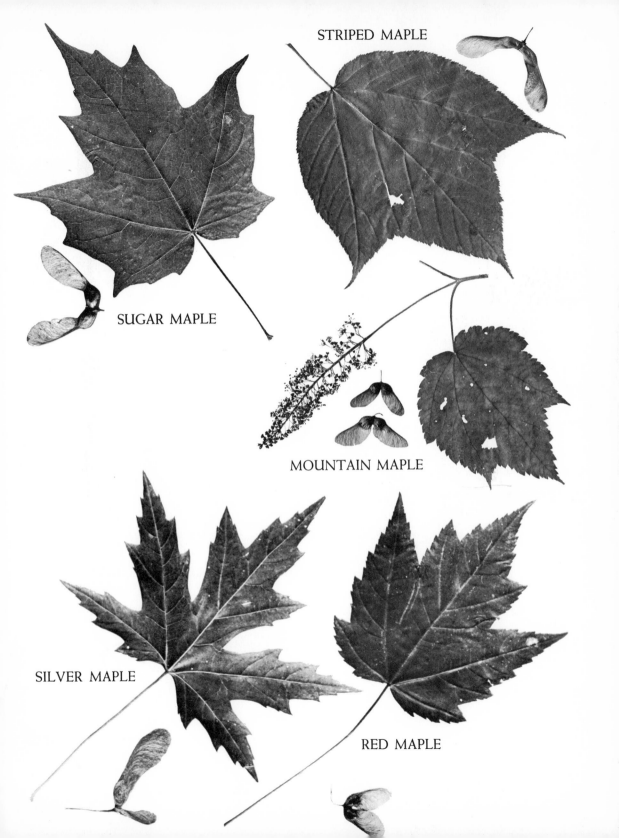

STRIPED MAPLE

SUGAR MAPLE

MOUNTAIN MAPLE

SILVER MAPLE

RED MAPLE

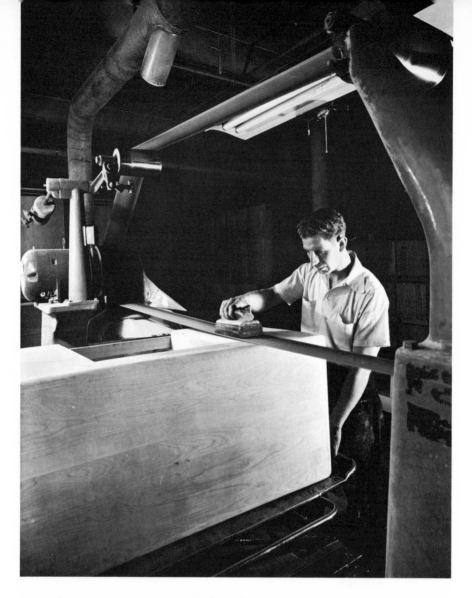

Maple trees are useful. Their wood is tough and strong. A lot of furniture is made out of it.

Maple syrup and maple sugar come from the sap of the sugar maple. The sap is ninety-seven percent water and has to be boiled down to produce syrup and sugar.

Maple trees are beautiful too.

## ABOUT THE AUTHOR

Millicent E. Selsam's career has been closely connected with biology and botany. She majored in biology and was graduated *magna cum laude* with a B.A. degree from Brooklyn College. At Columbia she received her M.A. in the Department of Botany, and since then has passed all course requirements and a comprehensive examination for a Ph.D., also at Columbia. After teaching biology for ten years in the New York City high schools, she has devoted herself to writing science books for children.

Mrs. Selsam and her husband live in New York City and spend their summers on Fire Island, New York.


## ABOUT THE PHOTOGRAPHER

Jerome Wexler was born in New York City, where he attended Pratt Institute. Later he studied at the University of Connecticut. His interest in photography started when he was in the ninth grade. After service in World War II, he worked for the State Department in Europe as a photographer. Returning to the United States, he specialized in photographing advanced farming techniques, and the pictures he made have been published throughout the world. When he became interested in nature photography some five years ago, he could not find equipment suited to his needs, so he designed and built his own with which he can photograph living plants and insects ten times their life size.

Mr. Wexler lives, with his wife and two children, in Yalesville, Connecticut.